I0142854

GOLDEN FEATHER

CHALLENGE

DEBBIE STRUCK

innovo
PUBLISHING

Published by Innovo Publishing, LLC
www.innovopublishing.com
1-888-546-2111

innovo
PUBLISHING

Providing Full-Service Publishing Services for Christian Authors, Artists &
Ministries: Hardbacks, Paperbacks, eBooks, Audiobooks, Music, Screenplays &
Curricula

The GOLDEN FEATHER CHALLENGE:
A QUEST FOR MANHOOD

Copyright © 2021 by D.R. Struck.
All rights reserved.

To learn more about the author, visit
JustFlipTheScript.com

No part of this publication may be reproduced, stored in a retrieval system, or
transmitted in any form or by any means electronic, mechanical,
photocopying, recording, or otherwise, without the prior written permission of
the author.

ISBN: 978-1-61314-634-7

Cover Design & Interior Layout: Innovo Publishing, LLC

Printed in the United States of America
U.S. Printing History
First Edition: 2021

Dedication

This Challenge is dedicated to my 3 little men whom I will always see as babies, but respect as warriors. Grant, Garrett & Levi are the fire behind this vision, the answer to so many prayers, and the living legacy that is altering the future of our entire family tree. As of the printing of this book, they are 19, 17, and 13 (respectively).

The path set before them is well planned by a mighty God, and the power that comes from knowing who they are and whose they are will never be defeated. Be of good courage, my sons.

Contents

Preface

When my son, Garrett, was 9 years old, he asked for his first pocket knife. I was confident that he was mature enough to understand safety and proper use of the knife, but I was concerned that he might not be responsible enough to keep up with it. I needed a test that would prove that he was ready before giving him his first knife.

I found a golden feather pendant from a necklace in my jewelry box that was about the same size and shape of a pocket knife. I removed the chain and made a deal with him. He was to treat the golden feather just like the pocket knife, carrying it in his pocket, keeping up with it, and always being prepared to show it to me when I gave him a pop check. If he could keep up with it for one month, then he would prove to be ready to own his first knife.

The moment I presented him with that pocket knife with his name engraved on it, he beamed with pride. Not only did he receive his first knife, but he had proven to himself that he deserved it, because he earned it. I called and he rose, but in the end, it was what he proved to himself that was the game changer.

Thus, *The Golden Feather Challenge* is born.

You need to have a point in time where it is declared over you that the mindset of the child must end and the new mindset of a man must be embraced. The man inside must be called out of you, like the howl of an alpha male wolf to its young. A transformation of the mind must take place.

> *"When I was a child, I talked like a child, I thought like a child, I reasoned like a child. When I became a man, I put the ways of childhood behind me."*
>
> *I Corinthians 13:11*

I'm so thankful you're here. It's my prayer that God would redeem every second you spend on this challenge and help you answer the ultimate question: *Do I have what it takes to be a man?* May you be ever confident, yet humble, in the divine design and in whose image you bear. Peace be with you.

> *"Think not that humility is weakness; it shall supply the marrow of strength to thy bones. Stoop and conquer; bow thyself and become invincible."*
>
> —*Charles Spurgeon*

Instructions on How to Use this Book

1. Read through all of the Challenges like you would a menu at a restaurant. Familiarize yourself with them. You can work through the Challenges in any order you choose, with one exception: you must complete Challenge #12 before you start Challenge #13.

2. You'll notice that the Challenges are printed on the left side of the book and a page with lines on the right. This space is for you to write any significant information you feel is worthy of remembering on that particular Challenge.

3. The last half of the book is space for more journaling.

Things you may want to jot down:

- How you feel about the Challenge before you begin. Be honest. If you are anxious or scared, say so. If you are excited or bored or somewhere in between, say so
- Questions that come up during your Challenge
- Ideas of other skills you would like to explore as part of this process
- Any names, dates, stories, or conversations that impact you during your Challenge
- Notes on what worked and what didn't with different challenges
- How you feel after completing the challenge. Be honest. Are you glad you did something you were scared to do? Do you feel like you thought you would before you started? Why?

4. If there is a Challenge that you have already mastered, try to level up on that Challenge by amending it to a greater difficulty for yourself.

5. This Challenge is intended to be a year-long journey, but since the journey itself is the most important, go at your own pace.

6. Go to goldenfeatherchallenge.com and register as a Challenger. We want to encourage you on your journey!

7. Don't give up!

This Golden Feather Journal
Belongs To:

_____

(Print Full Name Here)

_____   _____

(Date Started)   (Date Completed)

_____

(Signature Here)

Challenge One

FIRE

Master 3 ways to start a fire using friction, spark, and the sun. Try different methods and practice patience.

"At times our own light goes out and is rekindled by spark from another person. Each of us has cause to think with deep gratitude of those who have lighted the flame within us."

—*Albert Schweitzer*

Challenge Two

TEACH

Once you have mastered the skill of starting a fire, teach someone else how to do it. Offering the gift of a skill is more valuable than any worldly possession. The true gift comes back to you two-fold when building others up.

"If you have knowledge, let others light their candles at it."
—*Thomas Fuller*

D. R. Struck

Challenge Three

HIKE

Spend a minimum of 3 days in the woods. Hike. Sleep under the stars. Get as many miles in as you can each day. Hydrate and fuel your body because you cannot function otherwise. Spend some time reflecting on your value as a created being from a mighty Creator.

"Don't ask yourself what the world needs, ask yourself what makes you come alive, because what the world needs are men who come alive."

—*John Eldredge*

Challenge Four

SERVE OTHERS

Offer a day of service to a friend, family member, or neighbor; but accept nothing in return for your efforts.

"We have to humble ourselves and the way you do that is by serving other people."

—*Tim Tebow*

Challenge Five

FIREWOOD

Learn to use an axe properly and chop firewood. Create a full cord which is a 4ft high x 4ft wide x 8ft long pile of wood. You may have to be resourceful in obtaining logs for this challenge. You can keep it, give it away, or sell it.

"Chop your own wood and it will warm you twice."

—Henry Ford

Challenge Six

PLANT A TREE

Now that you know the strength of a tree, plant one and nurture
its early beginnings.

"The creation of a thousand forests is in one acorn."
—Ralph Waldo Emerson

Challenge Seven

SAVINGS

Save $500 for an emergency fund. Define what an emergency might be so this money is safe from improper use.

"By failing to prepare you are preparing to fail."
—*Benjamin Franklin*

Challenge Eight

DONATE

After accomplishing your Savings Challenge, donate your next $100 to a charity of your choosing.

"You have not lived today until you have done something for someone who can never repay you."

—*John Bunyan*

D. R. Struck

Challenge Nine

FITNESS

Discipline begins in your mind and must become the master of your body. Set a physical fitness goal (examples: run a 5-minute mile, 15 pull-ups, bench press your weight). Record the date you begin, your progress along the way, and the date you reach your goal.

"No man has the right to be an amateur in the matter of physical training. It is a shame for a man to grow old without seeing the beauty and strength of which his body is capable."

—*Socrates*

Challenge Ten

BUILD

Build something useful and give it away. (Hint: look for a need and build the solution.)

"Never respect men merely for their riches, but rather for their philanthropy; we do not value the sun for its height, but for its use."

—*Gamaliel Bailey*

D. R. Struck

Challenge Eleven

LEADERSHIP

Organize a team of your peers to run in a 5K race for a cause of your choosing.

"If your actions inspire others to dream more, learn more, do more and become more, you are a leader."

—*John Quincy Adams*

D. R. Struck

Challenge Twelve

MENTOR

Identify your mentor(s). A mentor is someone who sees more talent and ability within you than you see in yourself and helps bring it out of you. This must be accomplished before your next challenge.

"A single conversation across the table with a wise man is better than 10 years mere study of books."

—*Henry Wadsworth Longfellow*

D. R. Struck

Challenge Thirteen

HARD THINGS

Attempt a project that seems too big for you. Something so challenging it will require God to succeed. Prove to yourself that you can do hard things! (Hint: this goal should NOT be easily attainable within your own strength or efforts.) Failure is an option and that will be okay. Warriors do not back down when the chance of failure is present. They press on anyway. Discuss your goal with your mentor.

"I'd rather attempt to be something great and fail than to attempt to do nothing and succeed."

—*Robert H. Schuller*

Challenge Fourteen

DEVOTION

Prepare for and lead a family devotion. Choose a scripture that resonates with you. Meditate and pray on it. Put to words how the scripture has brought meaning or understanding to something in your life and share it with your family.

"A leader is one who knows the way, goes the way, and shows the way."

—*John C. Maxwell*

Challenge Fifteen

CITIZENSHIP

Read Theodore Roosevelt's speech "Duties of American Citizenship." Memorize your favorite excerpt.

"Battle is the most magnificent competition which a human being can indulge. It brings out all that is best; it removes all that is base. All men are afraid in battle. The coward is the one who lets his fear overcome his sense of duty. Duty is the essence of manhood."

—George S. Patton

Challenge Sixteen

COOK A MEAL

Cook a full meal for your family. That means budget, plan, shop, pay for, cook, serve, and clean-up the entire meal.

"All great change in America begins at the dinner table."
—Ronald Reagan

_____

_____

_____

_____

_____

_____

_____

_____

_____

_____

_____

_____

_____

_____

_____

_____

_____

_____

_____

_____

_____

Challenge Seventeen

VOLUNTEER

Volunteer in your community. Organize a project or join in with one that has already been organized.

"Try not to become a man of success, but a man of value. Look around at how people want to get more out of life than they put in. A man of value will give more than he receives."

—Albert Einstein

Challenge Eighteen

BATTLE PLAN

Memorize Psalm 91. This is your battle plan.

"Adversity toughens manhood, and the characteristic of good or the great man is not that he has been exempt from the evils of life, but that he has surmounted them."

—*Patrick Henry*

Challenge Nineteen

CONSIDER

Life is something that happens to me (thinking like a child)

vs.

Life is shaped by my decisions (thinking like a man)

This is a Challenge that will require quiet contemplation. Spend some time reflecting and define for yourself what a "life well lived" would look like for you. Write it down so you can remind yourself of the path you hope to remain upon.

"I don't want to have lived in vain like most people. I want to be useful or bring enjoyment to all people, even those I've never met. I want to go on living after my death!"

—*Anne Frank*

Challenge Twenty

READ

Read "Art of War" by Sun Tzu.

"Once you learn to read, you will be forever free."
—*Frederick Douglas*

Challenge Twenty-One

FAIL

Get comfortable with failure. Do not fear it. Do not let it stop you. Trials and failures grow us more than our triumphs. These are the defining moments in our lives, and there will be plenty of opportunity to see yourself through the lens of adversity. Use the remaining pages to record those things that cause you the greatest struggle. Those are the things that become the fuel in your journey to manhood and beyond.

"The ultimate measure of a man is not where he stands in moments of comfort and convenience, but where he stands at times of challenge and controversy."
—*Martin Luther King, Jr.*

If

By Rudyard Kipling

If you can keep your head when all about you
Are losing theirs and blaming it on you;
If you can trust yourself when all men doubt you,
But make allowance for their doubting too;
If you can wait and not be tired by waiting,
Or, being lied about, don't deal in lies,
Or, being hated, don't give way to hating,
And yet don't look too good, nor talk too wise;

If you can dream—and not make dreams your master;
If you can think—and not make thoughts your aim;
If you can meet with triumph and disaster
And treat those two impostors just the same;
If you can bear to hear the truth you've spoken
Twisted by knaves to make a trap for fools,
Or watch the things you gave your life to broken,
And stoop and build 'em up with wornout tools;

If you can make one heap of all your winnings
And risk it on one turn of pitch-and-toss,
And lose, and start again at your beginnings
And never breathe a word about your loss;
If you can force your heart and nerve and sinew
To serve your turn long after they are gone,
And so hold on when there is nothing in you
Except the Will which says to them: "Hold on";

If you can talk with crowds and keep your virtue,
Or walk with kings—nor lose the common touch;
If neither foes nor loving friends can hurt you;
If all men count with you, but none too much;
If you can fill the unforgiving minute
With sixty seconds' worth of distance run—
Yours is the Earth and everything that's in it,
And—which is more—you'll be a Man, my son!

Please visit goldenfeatherchallenge.com.

For many Challenges, the single journal page beside the Challenge will be all you need to capture your thoughts. However, for other Challenges, you may want to journal much more.

Use the pages that follow to capture your thoughts and feelings when you need more than one page. Just write the Challenge # and the date—and then make your journal entry. Do as many as you want.

When you look back on this years from now, you'll be thankful for taking the time now to capture more of your thoughts about each challenge.

Additional Journal Entries for Any Challenge

Additional Journal Entries for Any Challenge

Additional Journal Entries for Any Challenge

Additional Journal Entries for Any Challenge

_____

_____

_____

_____

_____

_____

_____

_____

_____

_____

_____

_____

_____

_____

_____

_____

_____

_____

_____

_____

Additional Journal Entries for Any Challenge

Additional Journal Entries for Any Challenge

Additional Journal Entries for Any Challenge

_____

_____

_____

_____

_____

_____

_____

_____

_____

_____

_____

_____

_____

_____

_____

_____

_____

_____

_____

_____

Additional Journal Entries for Any Challenge

Additional Journal Entries for Any Challenge

Additional Journal Entries for Any Challenge

_____

_____

_____

_____

_____

_____

_____

_____

_____

_____

_____

_____

_____

_____

_____

_____

_____

_____

_____

_____

_____

_____

_____

Additional Journal Entries for Any Challenge

Additional Journal Entries for Any Challenge

Additional Journal Entries for Any Challenge

Additional Journal Entries for Any Challenge

_____

_____

_____

_____

_____

_____

_____

_____

_____

_____

_____

_____

_____

_____

_____

_____

_____

_____

_____

_____

_____

Additional Journal Entries for Any Challenge

Additional Journal Entries for Any Challenge

Additional Journal Entries for Any Challenge

Additional Journal Entries for Any Challenge

Additional Journal Entries for Any Challenge

Additional Journal Entries for Any Challenge

Additional Journal Entries for Any Challenge

Additional Journal Entries for Any Challenge

Additional Journal Entries for Any Challenge

Additional Journal Entries for Any Challenge

_____

_____

_____

_____

_____

_____

_____

_____

_____

_____

_____

_____

_____

_____

_____

_____

_____

_____

_____

_____

_____

_____

Additional Journal Entries for Any Challenge

Additional Journal Entries for Any Challenge

Additional Journal Entries for Any Challenge

Additional Journal Entries for Any Challenge

Additional Journal Entries for Any Challenge

Additional Journal Entries for Any Challenge

Additional Journal Entries for Any Challenge

Additional Journal Entries for Any Challenge

Additional Journal Entries for Any Challenge

Additional Journal Entries for Any Challenge

Additional Journal Entries for Any Challenge

Additional Journal Entries for Any Challenge

Additional Journal Entries for Any Challenge

Additional Journal Entries for Any Challenge

Additional Journal Entries for Any Challenge

Additional Journal Entries for Any Challenge

_____

_____

_____

_____

_____

_____

_____

_____

_____

_____

_____

_____

_____

_____

_____

_____

_____

_____

_____

_____

_____

_____

_____

Additional Journal Entries for Any Challenge

Additional Journal Entries for Any Challenge

Additional Journal Entries for Any Challenge

Additional Journal Entries for Any Challenge

Additional Journal Entries for Any Challenge

Additional Journal Entries for Any Challenge

Additional Journal Entries for Any Challenge

Additional Journal Entries for Any Challenge

Additional Journal Entries for Any Challenge

Additional Journal Entries for Any Challenge

Additional Journal Entries for Any Challenge

Additional Journal Entries for Any Challenge

_____

_____

_____

_____

_____

_____

_____

_____

_____

_____

_____

_____

_____

_____

_____

_____

_____

_____

_____

_____

_____

_____

Additional Journal Entries for Any Challenge

Additional Journal Entries for Any Challenge

Additional Journal Entries for Any Challenge

Additional Journal Entries for Any Challenge

Additional Journal Entries for Any Challenge

Additional Journal Entries for Any Challenge

Additional Journal Entries for Any Challenge

Additional Journal Entries for Any Challenge

Additional Journal Entries for Any Challenge

Additional Journal Entries for Any Challenge

Additional Journal Entries for Any Challenge

_____

_____

_____

_____

_____

_____

_____

_____

_____

_____

_____

_____

_____

_____

_____

_____

_____

_____

_____

_____

_____

Additional Journal Entries for Any Challenge

Additional Journal Entries for Any Challenge

Additional Journal Entries for Any Challenge

Additional Journal Entries for Any Challenge

Additional Journal Entries for Any Challenge

Additional Journal Entries for Any Challenge

Additional Journal Entries for Any Challenge

Additional Journal Entries for Any Challenge

_____

_____

_____

_____

_____

_____

_____

_____

_____

_____

_____

_____

_____

_____

_____

_____

_____

_____

_____

_____

_____

Additional Journal Entries for Any Challenge

Additional Journal Entries for Any Challenge

Additional Journal Entries for Any Challenge

Additional Journal Entries for Any Challenge

_____

_____

_____

_____

_____

_____

_____

_____

_____

_____

_____

_____

_____

_____

_____

_____

_____

_____

_____

_____

_____

_____

Additional Journal Entries for Any Challenge

Additional Journal Entries for Any Challenge

Additional Journal Entries for Any Challenge

Additional Journal Entries for Any Challenge

Additional Journal Entries for Any Challenge

Additional Journal Entries for Any Challenge

Additional Journal Entries for Any Challenge

Additional Journal Entries for Any Challenge

Additional Journal Entries for Any Challenge

_____

_____

_____

_____

_____

_____

_____

_____

_____

_____

_____

_____

_____

_____

_____

_____

_____

_____

_____

_____

_____

Additional Journal Entries for Any Challenge

Additional Journal Entries for Any Challenge

Additional Journal Entries for Any Challenge

Additional Journal Entries for Any Challenge

Additional Journal Entries for Any Challenge

www.ingramcontent.com/pod-product-compliance
Lightning Source LLC
La Vergne TN
LVHW021503080426
835509LV00018B/2379